BS"D

THE BOOKBINDER
*A Personal Journey with the
Tzaddik Rabbi Yitzhak Kaduri, zt'l*

**By
Batya M. Goldman, Ph.D.**

The author dedicates this work
To the memory of

Rabbi Ralph Zebulun Glixman, z"l

A man who was a door of light for all who sought refuge in the Torah.

The life of a *tzaddik* is not a life of the flesh, but a spiritual life consisting wholly of faith, awe, and love of G-d.
—*Iggeret Hakodesh 27*

Acknowledgment

For a number of years we have been searching for our dear friends, Mr. & Mrs. Rosen through our contacts. Although we are now in the States and across the seas, we wish to thank them for having opened the window to an incredible chapter of our lives – living and learning about the Tsaddik Rabbi Yitzhak Kaduri, z'l. We owe them a debt of gratitude for having helped us when we needed guidance with our few earthly concerns. Mrs. "R" was a messenger to a great but humble man. Our wish is that they and their family be blessed by the Almighty with many joys, now and for years to come.

INDEX

Preface	11
Introduction	17
Aliyah	21
A Willing Driver	29
Trying Everything	43
The Tsaddik's Watchful Eye	51
Fulfilled and Complete	67
The Tsaddik's Promise of Moschiach	83
Forever with us	89
The Tsaddik's Dream	93
Looking Back	99
The Rebbe's Life	105

PREFACE

Since our return to the States in 2008, I have been impressed with the many inspired individuals that I have come across in our vibrant Jewish community of Miami. Many of them have something important to share, something that is worth learning to help us draw closer to our faith and way of life. I believe in heroes; I believe in men and women that do their work diligently without any fanfare. We need more people that will inspire us to live our lives in harmony with our traditions. It has been said that Rabbi Kaduri left no writings of his own. It is true that he endorsed a few prayer books edited by other scholar rabbis or funded by some of his devoted followers but nothing was written by him.

Recently I came across an article on the internet mentioning that a book was written by his students, *HaRav Kaduri*, and I am certain it is a faithful account of their experiences and the rabbi's lessons. This effort, however, is by no means scholarly. Rather, it is meant to be a more personal descriptive telling of his insight and kindness from our limited experience in a short few years. Who is to say that we are the right people to say anything about the rebbe? But, he was a hero to some and the hope of many thousands of countless followers within and without Israel, both Jewish and non-Jewish alike.

It is my prayer that this small endeavor will lead people to understand that the rebbe's soul has never been more powerful than it is today. The rebbe lived his Torah everyday and I can think of no better reason to tell this story than to show that it is necessary to have faith in something. We need more belief in the good, and it is crucial to always hope for the best. *Tsaddikim* (holy individuals) are examples of humble and pious men and women that take advantage of every breath to fulfill G-d's mitzvahs, to help a fellow Jew, to guide the lost, and do all this while no one is looking. Tsaddikim are holy especially because they do not call for the death or punishment of sinners just because they do not agree with any faith but rather work tirelessly to bring harmony between differing perspectives, traditions and sectors.

Readers may be surprised that I titled this book "The Bookbinder" when referring to the Tsaddik Rabbi Yitzhak Kaduri. My intention is to pay respect to a man whose humility was and should be an example to all religious and spiritual leaders both in Israel and beyond it.

One of the rebbe's first jobs in the Holy Land was to bind the books and manuscripts at the Porat Yosef Yeshiva. Yet what I remember of the tsaddik, in the decade we were privileged to be in his presence, is that although his work was the study of the Talmud, the Tanach and its secrets, his true mission was to protect Am Israel and bind it to the Torah.

When young couples, worried parents, grieving widows and anyone in need of spiritual uplifting came to see the tsaddik because of their personal tragedies the rebbe would "bind" them to the Torah through prayer, he would instruct them on how to pray with devotion and faith, and he would bless them so that their success would be tied to a greater love and understanding of Judaism and spiritual growth.

No one ever came away sad or feeling hopeless after seeing him. That is because he knew how to bind souls to the Torah, to its teachings and to its blessings.

Binding books is a complicated and delicate task given to those very special individuals that have the patience and love for the Holy Scriptures and at the same time strive to preserve its body of teachings for the enrichment of generations to come. The same can be said for the reverence and compassion needed to care for Am Israel. It was not a job for just anyone. In this sense, our tsaddik, Rabbi Kaduri, was the holiest of "bookbinders".

May our Creator accept this work as our humble offering of love and devotion to His commandments and to one of His teachers – the "Rav".

The author

Introduction

Nine years ago, on January 28th, 2006, the Tsaddik Rabbi Yitzhak Kaduri, (OBM), ascended to meet the Creator. When our family left Israel in 1999 due to my husband's work demands, we felt that part of our heart was left behind in Eretz haKodesh (Holy Land). When we took a sabbatical and left for the United States, we immediately went to visit the tsaddik. We implored and wept in his presence, asking him what was the meaning of this return to America? When we had made aliyah in 1991, it was meant to be permanent. We recall his reply to us; "You leave by the "*chesed*" (kindness) of the Almighty, and when you return, it will be a stronger and more blessed homecoming." It was left up to us to understand and interpret his words of wisdom. In 2016, the tsaddik would have lived nigh close to his 120's. It was rumored, although never truly confirmed in order to protect his life, that he lived well into 112 years old. I was sure that he would live to our Prophet Moses' years. Yet I believe that the sacrifice of surrendering his life to protect our beautiful Israel was more important.

Both the tsaddik and the prime minister at the time, the late Prime Minister Ariel Sharon, both succumbed to illness almost in symphony. Although "Arik" fell into a coma that lasted until 2014, the tsaddik's journey ended in 2006.

This book is written in homage to our master and teacher. He did not instruct us, the little people, in a classroom but by example. He rarely spoke but only when he prayed or when he was counseling someone. We know from our own experience that he never socialized or chatted with any person but only spoke with substance. It is legendary knowledge that in his youth the tsaddik had been instructed to limit his speech to holy endeavors and he followed that instruction to his last day. In the many events that we participated, in the many charities and fundraisers that were held to support his kollel, in between speeches from other rabbis, our tsaddik would sit quietly reading and praying. He rarely spoke but when he did it was to give a blessing. His teachings were passed on by those close to him, and by his kabbalist rabbis that studied and practiced under his rigorous guidance. The tsaddik shunned both publicity and popularity. He disliked photographers and knew the dangers of his image being published. His was only one mission, protect Am Israel and the small but fiercely strong nation that it is today. We are forever grateful to the messenger and friend that joined us to his court, Mrs. N. Rosen and her wonderful down-to-earth husband, T. Rosen.

Our life was changed by his words, by his blessings, by his visits, and by his kindness. In fact, who were we to have been favored by his glance? No one can answer that, but the tsaddik's teachings of love, tolerance, *"emuna"* (faith), peace and strength will remain with us and our family for the ages.

I write of our short life with him to honor his actions, his beliefs, and because our tsaddik, Rabbi Yitzhak Kaduri, was in life and is even greater in spirit after his passing, a force of nature!

May the memory of our teacher be eternal, may his soul still expound in the heavenly courts in Am Israel's favor and his grace touch us all in our hour of need.

Batya M. Goldman

ALIYAH

In 1987, in my hometown of Miami, FL, through my work at a cruise line office, I met the man that would be my best friend for life, Ariel. We met in the US offices of a large Italian cruise company. After three long years of avoiding his invitations to go out for coffee, I finally relented. I had always been very private about my personal life and as a single mother I worked two jobs in order to make ends meet. There really wasn't time or interest on my part to socialize so it was very easy to say "no" for so long. I'm grateful that we finally went out for coffee in the winter of 1989. In 1990, Ariel and I were married by Rabbi Ralph Z. Glixman (zl), in a small religious ceremony in his synagogue and community in Homestead, FL.

Our rebbe, Rabbi Glixman, was from the Chassidic Gur family. Although the rabbi was tall and with a heavy build, he was gentle as he was warm and welcoming. The Shabbats spent at his *schul* in Homestead were memorable. The Jewish observant families that chose to stay overnight at the synagogue would come early to prepare their sleeping arrangements. There was nothing more exciting than sitting at the rebbe's table on Friday nights and listening to that week's parshah reading. The rebbe would intersperse the lessons with his own insights. We had many observant families that chose to spend their weekends at the schul and Torah-related conversations lasted well into the late hours of the night. The young children would run around and play together until midnight while the men learned Torah somewhere in another corner of the schul's open spaces. Sometimes the wives would ask the rebbe to give us a lesson on anything special that he considered important for us. We loved sitting around the table listening to the rabbi's wisdom, and we were always thirsty for more. The rabbi would always cap his teachings with one of his most important tenets, something that we have carried with us to this day. It was probably his most basic teaching when trying to reach out to the many young people, the young couples and families that came from differing shades of religious commitment. He always taught; *"Ein dati, ein heloni, esh rak yehudi"*. It translates as: "there are no religious and no secular, there is only a Jew" and it was a teaching that he received from his rabbinical teachers. With that directive we were taught to always respect, honor and love the fellow Jew in our midst devoid of judgment, devoid of prejudice, and devoid of religious arrogance. The rebbe felt strongly that this type of negative thinking was the underpinnings of the Holocaust, the destruction of our Holy Temple as well as the Inquisition. As a family we have tried to embody that concept and live with this message in everything we do. Even after we moved to Israel, the rebbe and his family were always close to us even if most of the time it was via the telephone.

When we first married we settled in Kendall, Florida. We always had our eye on one day making aliyah (a term that means "ascending" to the Holy Land). My husband travelled extensively to Europe and spent there many weeks at a time due to his work. After a few of these long stretches of time away from home, I made it clear that this wasn't what I wanted for our family life. Something had to change. Thinking about this long and hard we decided that moving to Israel instead of Europe would be easier on the family. It was true that I'd be apart from my parents but I hoped that in the future they would come visit us. In 1991 we were expecting our second daughter, Batel. Whatever needed to be done to make "aliyah" had to happen that year. And so it was that on June 23rd of 1991, we moved to Israel. It goes without saying that this was also the most exciting time of our lives; Ariel was returning to his native country after a 20 year absence and, I was finally fulfilling my dream of living in Israel. We felt as if we had won the lottery.

Aliyah in 1991

When we arrived to Israel - at the beginning - we lived in Ariel's parents' home in Tel Aviv. This was a small 85 square meter apartment – picture for yourself the dimensions of a one-bedroom home! My mother-in-law was thrilled that we were now living with her and since we lived in the center of Tel-Aviv, there was little need for a car. My daughter Tati was adjusting to her new school and her *ulpan* (language institute) and I was busy making preparations for our new baby's arrival.

We lived with Mama Claire for six months before we found a home to rent in Ramat Hasharon. One year after that we finally moved to our favorite city, Ra'anana, into a beautiful country house overlooking orange groves. I had always loved the country-side and the angels must have heard my prayers because we were able to find a new home that had never been leased. Some of our happiest memories were made in that house and we lived there for five years. It was during that time that life began to change for me.

Severe Illness

Again my husband's work continued to take him out of the country for two to three weeks at a time, but then it was easier because he was only three hours away by plane and not dealing with the jet lag of intercontinental travel. Together, Tati and I tried to make our lives as holistic, natural and active as possible. Living in the countryside was always less expensive and far more relaxing. Tati began riding lessons nearby because there were a good number of stables in the area. Horseback riding was not a sport reserved for the rich but rather for the nature loving residents. In time we were able to surprise her with her own ride, Mistral, a 15-hand auburn red Hanoverian mare with a gentle disposition for children. When my husband travelled, we would spend most of our time after school either at the stable or outdoors. On several occasions I came down with severe bouts of bronchial asthma which, if left unchecked, would develop into more serious respiratory infections. Although we lead a healthy life and ate wholesome foods, still, the simple fact that I had no family other than my mother-in-law was quite stressful for all of us. Tati and now, Batel, our new baby, were the focus of my life and there has never been a greater joy but I missed my parents and my life back home.

I became sick more and more often until the bronchitis escalated to pneumonia. The first time I developed it, my husband had to stop travelling to care for the girls and me. I've always been self-reliant and a pioneer with anything that I took a mind to do. Not happy with being sick, I would avoid going to the doctor until I wore myself out until it was too late. When I finally came down with pneumonia, our physician said that I needed bed rest for at least one week. One week! That was impossible, there was so much to do, the baby to care for, Tati's school lessons and the house to look after – whoever heard of a mother parking herself for one week in bed? After one week we thought it had all but disappeared and I started moving around again. But after another two weeks, I collapsed. My poor little girl Tati, at the age of 9, was left to call the emergency services because I could barely breathe from my bronchitis and Ariel was not home. Our physician was seriously worried now and emphasized the need for me to have someone at home because this second time could bring about another infection. In 1993 alone I suffered two bouts of debilitating pneumonia.

A WILLING DRIVER

The Un-named Tsaddik

My husband had several good friends in Tel-Aviv, and one of them introduced him to a very special lady by the name of Mrs. N. Rosen. Of Jewish-Iraqi origins, she was a happy, over-nurturing and caring woman that was always helping others either directly or connecting them with others that could provide the help. She spoke Hebrew and Arabic because of her upbringing in the Iraqi neighborhood of Ramat Gan. After having met briefly at a wedding reception, N. would periodically check in with us to see how we and the girls were doing. Although with grown-up children of her own, she seemed to always have time to listen and had a bag full of magical solutions for anyone that needed help, a prayer or blessing from her rabbi. Always on the lookout for the latest prayer book or the latest news on some other kabbalist rabbi (tzaddik) in Jerusalem said to perform miracles with his prayers, N. was tireless when it came to looking out for a person's health and well being. I could fill volumes with the names of the many needy individuals that asked her for prayers for prosperity, for a job, for a life mate (shidduch), for recovery from cancer or any other serious concern. N. Rosen never turned away anyone asking for help, "no" was not part of her vocabulary.

One evening she was heading up to Jerusalem from Tel Aviv to visit her rabbi and offered to ask him for a blessing to heal me. She asked us if we allowed her to give the rabbi my name for a blessing. Ariel said of course, anything that would help was more than welcome. We assured her that the next time we'd see her we would repay her gesture by giving a tzedaka (donation) to be given to a needy person. At least once a week our friend and her husband T. would make the 45 minute drive from Tel

Aviv to Jerusalem to visit her sainted rabbi and mentor. On those visits she would sit with her husband and the rabbi and rabbanit in their humble apartment inside the kollel (house of study) and quietly drink tea. At the time Ariel and I were so busy with my health concerns that we never thought to ask our kind friend who she was going to visit.

The Blessing and the Gift

That night N. asked her rabbi for a blessing on my behalf. As is usual and typical, most rabbis simply ask for the person's first name and mother's name. This rabbi was more meditative than most in his position. This is because he was a kabbalist. Once given my name N. said that he deliberately paused – as he usually did when investigating something serious - as if he was listening to the angels. That night, while praying for me, he turned and asked N. if she had any piece of jewelry in her possession that wasn't needed and that didn't belong to her. N. replied that yes, of course - what a coincidence! - in her purse there was a golden ring that was sent as a gift to the rabbi and she had meant to give it to him before she left. The rabbi said that he needed to place a blessing over the ring and have it immediately delivered to our home. The rabbi assured N. that I would recuperate from this serious illness and would soon get up from bed. Our friend observed his urgency and focus and obeyed his instructions – to ensure the delivery of the blessed ring.

The next morning, a messenger from N.'s office knocked on our door and hand delivered a small package that had been brought back by our friend from Jerusalem. Ariel immediately came upstairs to the bedroom and told me that this ring came from a very holy person in Jerusalem. Strange enough, we could still not remember the rabbi's name. Since N. was always helping others she knew plenty of people all over Israel. She wanted to make sure that the recovery would be permanent and told us that she knew of a physical therapist and friend that lived near our town that was experienced in working with respiratory illnesses. She recommended her therapist friend to us and suggested that perhaps in a few weeks after I was over the worst part of my convalescence, her friend therapist could come visit me for a few treatments.

I want to say at this juncture that I have always had faith in a person's good intentions. Maybe that's the way I'm built, but I don't immediately think the worst of people. In this particular case, with the delivery of the blessed ring, neither I nor my husband could have understood what occurred that day. Since we were not familiar with the work of kabbalists, only rabbis, we did not understand the import of the tzaddik's blessing. All that I know and remember is that on that morning, while still lying in bed, weak and tired, Ariel came over and handed me the small box and asked me to put the ring on my finger. It was both his hope and mine that I would soon be feeling better. I can't begin to tell you how much medications, antibiotics and tonics had been administered in the days leading up to my health crisis, but I can assure you that after days of seeing no improvement, the next step threatened to be hospitalization and in an oxygen tent!

Ariel spoon fed me his home-made chicken-soup and hoped that perhaps I might be able to sit up that day. The days and nights before that day seemed to join in a blur, and I could only mark the afternoons because that's when our daughter Tati would come back from school. Little Batel was waddling in her crib and every now and then she would call out to us to come and get her. Poor Ariel was stressed, I was tired and the girls were anxious to get back to their old routines. That late afternoon I finally sat up in bed without coughing my lungs out or feeling that terrible searing pain. Of course the chicken soup helped to strengthen my immune system, but having been in bed for so many days seemed to make my legs feel like wet noodles.

On this day, I seemed to have a little strength to lift my shoulders from the pillow and turn my head to look out the window. I was grateful to be alive, and I was even more thankful that I could breathe easier than before. Still not connecting the dots, I managed to get up slowly from my bed, and walk a few steps to shower. In one day I was able to keep down some liquid, walk a few steps and wash. The miracles had already begun.

Friends Helping Friends

As the days passed I regained my strength, and with it, the faith that something amazing had just happened to us. N. would call us every day to check on my progress and then report back to the rabbi about my recovery. All the time we did not know anything about the rabbi's tight circle of devotees, students and family. All we knew is that he had reached out to us through someone that he loved and respected as a daughter which also happened to be our friend – N. After a few weeks, when I was strong enough to move around and eat normally, life took its normal course again. The girls were happy, Ariel was working and travelling again and I was working hard not to repeat old mistakes.

During the two weeks that Ariel was home, he decided to reach out to our friend and ask her for the contact details of her therapist friend. "Of course!" said N., give her a call, she'll be happy to come by and see you. If you like the way she works maybe she can give your wife therapy more than once a week. Believe me when I tell you, she has magic hands."
That is all she said.

That night we reached out to our new-found therapist, Dahlia. She was warm, friendly and funny. She appreciated that N. had recommended her to us and she seemed to understand exactly what therapy was needed in order to make sure that I didn't get sick again.

Dahlia N. did visit us that week and Ariel and I felt very reassured after her very first session. She was gentle, compassionate and a very caring professional. She was a good listener and intuitive as to the best way to be proactive about my respiratory problems. I never felt better than when she treated me and I looked forward to her weekly visits.

So, we were happily surprised when she asked us if we would join her on her weekly trip to Jerusalem. When we inquired, Dahlia mentioned that she didn't like to drive at night and was usually accompanied by N. and whoever volunteered to drive them up to Jerusalem. When we asked her where we'd be taking her, she quietly responded that we were going to "the tzaddik's home" in the Bukharian Quarter. We asked Dahlia who was this tsaddik that she treated on a weekly basis and she stated "It's THE tsaddik, Rabbi Yitzhak Kaduri". We were still no wiser by the name. In 1992, there was very little internet outside of e-mail accounts and there was literally nothing written anywhere about a lot of things – let alone about this quiet, unassuming rabbi.

The days prior to our driving Dahlia up to Jerusalem, we asked our friends if they had ever heard of this rabbi. We were surprised about their reaction. Our acquaintances, in surprise, would relate some of the miracles he was known for, others would explain how many people were willing to wait in long lines every day outside of his little flat to get a brief interview with the saint. It was hard to plumb the depths of the subject, although we kept everything pretty quiet, our friends would explain that this rabbi was the final authority when two major rabbis disputed over halachic matters. Others would relate how far people travelled to see him and how costly it could be to finally obtain a visit with this kabbalist. All the time my husband and I just kept quiet. First of all, we were humbled that we would get the opportunity to drive his therapist to treat him as this was a mitzvah equal in value as one who visits the sick, "*bikkur holim*". Secondly, we were in awe at how strange life had arranged it that we would soon enter his private home. I think back on those days and wonder how we were not more scared than what we already were. Maybe it was a strange case of "ignorance is bliss". Only time would reveal to us how truly young and inexperienced we were in these matters.

Our First Tea

Dahlia called to confirm that we'd be picking her and N. up on that Tuesday to head for Jerusalem. Since the rabbi studied until late at the kollel, we would head out from Ra'anana by 7:30pm to arrive by 8:30 or 9:00pm. The later one arrived, the better it was for the rabbi and his wife. The rabbi and his wife dined early as was his practice. We would arrive in time to join them for tea. On the way there we chatted about N.'s long list of request for prayers and queries from friends and family members. I marveled at how every opportunity to reach the rabbi was optimized by these kind women. Upon arrival we saw that during the first half of the visit, the rabbi was ushered to his room to be treated by the therapist – in company of his wife, Rabbanit Dorit.

Many in his court were opposed to this marriage, but it was her humility and devotion that melted everyone's heart. No one dared oppose the tsaddik's decisions, and when he waited the prescribed time after the passing of his first wife, he chose R. Dorit among many because of her peaceful and gentle demeanor. It was halachically appropriate that a rabbi remarry, and this rabbi and kabbalist above all, could read the hearts of his court. There was no kinder woman for this privilege. She spoke softly, barely making any noise, and always seemed to be quick on her feet. I don't recall that she ever sat down with us but rather was always bustling about in the kitchen and serving tea to all of the rebbe's guests. She was a tireless woman, devoted to her husband, and his well-being was her main concern.

When we first entered his humble abode one would never have believed that this was the home of the sage of sages of the time. With a long hall from the front door that opened into a long dining room area, we noticed there was no living room area. There was only a very long table, close to four meters long, covered with a white tablecloth from end to end.

Here, at this table, sat many scholars seeking clarification of a law or ruling from the tsaddik. Here, many poor yeshiva students would come to pray with the rabbi. Here, many private citizens gladly made donations in any amount of money just to hear the tsaddik's words of hope and solace. At this table, many discussed the teachings of even greater rabbis of the past. And, when the tsaddik avidly read and prayed, he rarely lifted his eyes to see who had entered the room to sit at the table of guests. Because, here all men were equal in value, all were welcome, but all knew well that he did not suffer gossip or judgment of another.

You might wonder how we learned this so quickly but it was only because at our first meeting with the tsaddik and his wife, we had time to look around the table and noticed that it was surrounded on three sides by tall, wooden, deep bookshelves holding some of the most precious books and manuscripts in existence. This was an permanent place of study. And this evening, while we quietly entered through the door into the dining room, we could feel the peace and tranquility, the sacredness of the place, even though it was now empty of scholars and students.

The rabbanit quickly brought us glasses of strong tea and biscuits while we waited for his arrival. While hosting us, she explained that the days could be long if these scholars needed to resolve a matter. Here, at this table, they vied for his favor, they hoped to hear his opinions, and his rulings were capped with insight and awe of the Almighty. The visitors hoped to touch his leftovers, as has been a long-standing custom that students eat from their master's plate. Here, sages prayed to be included in his discussions. No rabbi dared oppose his views. If they were balanced, they were also absolute. And, here at this table, my husband and I quietly sipped our tea in anticipation of the tsaddik's appearance.

When the rebbe appeared, we all got up to receive him. His mouth held a permanent smile, his eyes lit with illumination, and if you looked closely at his forehead, you could see that the subtle shape of the Hebrew letter "*Heh*" seemed to be folded into the creases of his brow. N. pointed out that this must have appeared years ago when he was still binding the holy books at his first job in a yeshiva, because Rabbi Kaduri was known to have a photographic memory. He forgot nothing. The rebbe was very tall, even though he was bent with a century of years on his shoulders, it seemed that he must have been extremely tall in his youth, standing a good two meters tall. So, when he was helped into his chair, he was still a presence to witness.

Looking at him I had a knot in my throat. Maybe I was impressed just by being there, but I know I couldn't speak a word. I felt that any Hebrew I knew had quickly vanished from my memory. I was a simple mute, just basking in the muted light of the room. I sat further down the end of the table behind my husband Ariel. All I could do was look and listen. N. began by asking him how he felt and if his therapy was good. She hoped that he was in good spirits for her so that she could ask him for blessings and prayers for the people on her list. He nodded, gently chuckled, and replied by making a blessing before sipping the tea. Although he never seemed to speak long sentences, when he spoke Arabic, N. would repeat his reply out loud just so that she would get his answer right.

The list went on for about 45 minutes and his blessings followed most of those requests. Thereafter he inquired the names of the person that had kindly brought Dahlia and N. to his home. N. gave the tsaddik my husband's name. He nodded in approval and blessed Ariel. N. also explained to the rabbi that I was the woman that he saved with the gift of the blessed ring. The tsaddik nodded. "Ah, he said, this is the driver's wife?" Again he chuckled in joy. Who would have told me a month before that on this evening I would be in the presence of this sage, a saint, a humble servant of Hashem, and a presence to witness? I vowed never to forget the experience.

We left their home close to midnight. Indeed it was time to leave, as the rabbi's schedule was strenuous. He would begin his prayers of *Tikun Hatzot* (Midnight Repairs) and then sleep until the early hours before dawn where at around 4:00am he would begin his dawn prayers *Shaharit* and his list of intentions.

That night we slept deep.

TRYING EVERYTHING

Great but short-lived success

In December of 1992, on the second day of Hannukah, I gave birth to our third daughter, Yardena, in Tel Aviv. We were joyous at the beautiful family we were building. Indeed, it seemed that most of my health concerns had become a distant and long forgotten chapter of my life.

After having tried for about two years to find employment in Israel, I decided to open our own business. My training and education permitted me to create something unique that hadn't been done before on a professional level and so, step by step, we carefully prepared to launch the Harry Goldman Institute, named after my father-in-law. Sir Goldman was a thermo-dynamic engineer, a pioneer in the early years of the formation of the State of Israel, and foremost an educated and cultured scientist listed in the world's "Who's Who" of Europe. We wanted to focus on those old-world and classic traditions and founded an institute of professional ethics and business etiquette. We invested a part of our savings and poured ourselves into the project and in truth, in 12 months, the curriculum that we prepared and the programs took off with complete and total success! There was only one problem – after having offered the programs to most of the first secretaries and Protocol Officers of the major universities, we seemed to run out of candidates. The program was successfully acclaimed in the Israeli press for many months.

Until we encountered our first industrial "spy". A woman who had held the contract for professional etiquette with the Ministry of Exterior for many years must have felt threatened by our success. She sent a student to take our course. In less than one week we discovered our program under the woman's name offering the identical concepts that we had worked so hard for. When we sought legal action we were advised that even if the material looked the same, it could never be instructed in the same fashion – as the teacher did not have the same experiences and background that we offered. Even still, it seemed that our business was headed for the rocks.

Do what you do best!

It was at this time, when I was expecting our first son, that we were considering closing down the business. We asked our friend N. Rosen to approach the tsaddik and ask him what could be done to save the business. His reply was amazing: "Do what you do best..... begin seeing people again, listen to them, and counsel them. You have done this with success and you must do it once more. You will succeed."

I thought I understood what the rebbe was referring to; I used to provide religious counseling and spiritual support to the enlisted personnel during my time in the U.S. Navy as an interdenominational chaplain, aside from my regular career. As a matter of history, together with two other colleagues at the time I founded a support group for single parents at one of my duty stations. It seemed that he might have senses this experience from having studied my name because I had not spoken with anybody about my previous work in the states. And so I began seeing clients from all walks of life that were in need of a good word or a hopeful perspective to confront their difficult life trials. I would begin the day by meditating on the Book of Psalms to gain valuable insight into the individual's concerns.

All of a sudden, my days were fully booked. I would begin seeing clients from 1:00pm until well into midnight everyday! Who would have thought this would have taken the turn it did? In the following weeks Rabbi Kaduri asked N. to send me a framed blessing for my work to be displayed in my work spaces. We were, again, humbled by his kindnesses and forethought. Of course, N. played a large part in helping us during this crisis because she had lived through our many financial difficulties and the loss of the institute would have affected us. Quickly, we returned some of the leased artwork to the galleries, sold off a large portion of the furniture, but kept only our extensive library. We had taken a risk, succeeded with the institute's goals, created a movement, and then quietly went away.

It was time to listen to the tsaddik again.

Mercaz Ruhanit – A Center for Prayer and Counseling

With a new found energy and the rebbe's blessing in our hands, we terminated our lease and searched for smaller spaces where we could receive the people that flocked our business. I never believed in advertising for this work because I had always seen it as a special mission. Believing that if I maintained the same level of deep conviction and a higher level of ethics, if the work was meant to survive, it would do so no matter where we would go. So we found a small apartment in a quiet residential area of Ra'anana and I continued meeting the many men and women, both religious and secular that were in need of guidance. But, primarily I saw in all of them a great need for hope and this we strived to give with every encounter. We were committed to helping others and when we felt that something warranted a greater level of halachic knowledge or rabbinical intervention, as many times did occur, we would direct the person to either contact our friend N. or search out an audience with the rebbe for accurate halachic authority. First and foremost he was our guide, our mentor, and his blessings and support were integral to any success that we experienced.

As a modern orthodox Jewish family, we made every effort to embody the principles of Judaism, devoid of judgment and prejudice. My husband Ariel and I saw our function as setting the example of always looking for the positive in every trial experienced and find the *"chesed"* provided by our Creator. An answer was always given to us in our hour of need, and this message was shared with every person that I met. As devoted followers of the rebbe, we heard and saw how he ruled and instructed those who came to him seeking answers and solutions to their problems. He approached all with understanding, love, an indescribable inner joy, and yet with firmness. It is true that he did this with a minimal amount of words – but then this was the rebbe's signature: talk little, do more. We learned from Rabbi Kaduri, and realized that as his followers, we could do no less.

In the fall of 1995, my mother-in-law, Mama Claire, gifted us with a sefer Torah, to be placed in the center. Because it was such a special occasion we inquired if it was possible that the rebbe would bless the installment of the Torah scroll in our center. The answer was a resounding yes! We were so excited about his acceptance to lead the prayers that we reached out to our own rebbe in Miami, Florida, Rabbi Ralph Z. Glixman, to please join us. It was a blessing for us that our hometown rabbi from Miami, Florida also accepted and was able to join us together with two of his sons, Ben-Zion and Ami Glixman.

The local papers and history showed that on September of 1995, Rabbi Yitzhak Kaduri, entered the city of Ra'anana, and celebrated the "hanukat bait" or inauguration of the Mercaz Ruhanit to welcome a new sefer Torah. The rebbe was welcomed and surrounded by the presence of the Chief Rabbi of the Municipality of Ra'anana, Rabbi Peretz and many other city dignitaries were in attendance for such an auspicious event.

Ariel and I felt grateful to the Almighty and blessed by this historical experience.

THE TSADDIK'S WATCHFUL EYE

The Tsaddik and Our Infant Son

Our son was born in Sukkoth of 1994, and it was a joyous occasion for our family but especially so for my husband. He was the only child of Claire and Sir Harry Goldman. It was natural that he would worry about progeny. Would he have a son to carry his name and to do kaddish when his time would come? Our prayers were answered.

We named him after my favorite biblical figure; King David, but gave him the middle name of Ariel's uncle, who had passed away during World War II while serving in the French Legion. His uncle was a medical doctor that had graduated from the University of Paris.

When we learned that I was carrying a son, suddenly I began to have dreams of a military officer that came to visit me. Since I had never seen a picture of Ariel's uncle I didn't know who this man was but he seemed earnestly joyous that I was carrying a son. In my dreams this gentleman would come for many weeks, sometimes we were walking down a street, sometimes sitting down at a table, or sometimes in a park. When I described him to my husband, Ariel felt that perhaps his uncle was coming into my dreams in order to show his happiness with the good tidings. In our enthusiasm we decided to add his uncle's name to our son.

The Miracle Visit

In 1995, our oldest daughter Tati was going to celebrate her bat-mitzvah joined by her siblings, her family and her classmates. We had flown my parents from the USA for the happy occasion and there was much excitement because they still had not met their youngest grandchild – David.

On the evening of the celebration, we all arrived at the banquet hall to prepare to receive the guests and family. David was just six months old and must have been running a fever for a while. We had checked with the family doctor days before and he couldn't find any reason for the infection but he asked us to keep an eye on the fever, which seemed not to subside. Our babysitter, Mali, tagged along and assured us she wouldn't let go of David all night.

As the night progressed both my husband and I would take turns holding David and when needed, my mother, *"abuela"*, would rock him in his stroller to lull him to sleep. Several hours into the celebration the baby wasn't getting better. Mali decided to pick him up and carry him outside to the hall and landing where there was a cool air flowing up the stairwell. Pacing back and forth with the baby in her arms, she noticed the figure of a man dressed in a white robe and white kippa descending the stairs. He stopped in front of Mali and said, "What is the child's name?", and Mali duly replied. He placed his hands on David's head and said, "Do not worry, the boy will be well." And, then he descended the stairs. Mali just noted that she didn't see his feet but was too busy rocking the baby. In minutes Mali noticed that David was no longer red and hot and when she touched his forehead, it seemed he was cool and had fallen asleep. She immediately climbed up the stairs and entered the hall where we sat and asked, "Who was the rabbi dressed in white that you invited?". Ariel and I looked at each other and shook our heads. We had not invited any rabbis to this small function and there was only one orthodox man who in fact, was dressed in a black coat and fur hat – not in white. We assured Mali that we didn't know anyone by that description.

Imagine the surprise when next morning Mali entered our house and noticed Ariel's family pictures on our mantelpiece. She ran to a small framed image of a young man dressed in the uniform of the French Legion. It was Ariel's deceased uncle. "That's the man that I met last night! That was him!". My husband explained that this wasn't possible because his uncle had died during WWII. Mali broke into tears fearing that we didn't believe her but actually – we did.

Blessings come in unique ways and we were no strangers to these spiritual occurrences. We credited this visit to the Almighty's watchful eye for we have always believed that everything comes from the Creator.

Visit to the Kollel

When David was eight months old, we asked N. if the tsaddik would give our son a blessing. It was not a request made out of need as our son was born healthy and was a happy and strong baby. N. and her husband smiled in delight and said of course – "let's bring him to the rebbe while he is studying upstairs in the kollel". That week we brought our son David to the tsaddik's place of study. We were ushered upstairs and together with N. and T., we waited quietly in the hall until someone came out and signaled to T. to bring our infant son inside.

The tsaddik was sitting in a tall wooden chair against a wall, while around him, in a circle sat his *mekubalim* (kabbalist students). T. placed our son on the rebbe's knees. It seemed so strange, this tall giant of a man, a truly inspiring sage that exuded quiet majesty, and here he was holding this six-month old baby boy. The rebbe gave him one finger for David to hold on to. The rebbe just chuckled and looked deeply at our son. We could barely see anything as we were asked to wait outside. Five, ten and fifteen minutes passed and still we didn't hear anything from inside. Finally we asked T. to check in on our son. T. assured us there was no reason to worry – the baby and the rebbe were very peaceful and content gazing at each other – David would pat the rebbe's long beard, and the rebbe just kept holding on to the small hand.

The *mekubalim* sat quietly observing their master while the master enjoyed a moment of innocence. We weren't allowed to take pictures of the moment, but I remember peeking in at the end and seeing David lifted from the rabbi's lap. N. and T. remarked that our baby had not cried or even whimpered, it seemed as though he was entirely at home in the presence of the rebbe. It seemed that the rabbi recognized someone in the soul (*neshama*) of our son.

The Tsaddik's Remarkable Conclusion

We would need many pages to describe the numerous trials that we underwent before David safely arrived to his third birthday. One of those precarious incidents took place during his first year. Our son was dropped by our mother's helper, a woman that unbeknownst to us suffered catatonic episodes. What saved him was that my husband had been standing near her and so he caught our baby in time. In another incident, at 18 months, David almost drowned while sitting at my feet in a wading pool where the water was no more than 4 inches high. I had noticed that I didn't feel his weight on my feet as he'd been splashing the water. When next I saw him he was floating face down on the shallow water. That particular time Ariel's father appeared to him and asked him "My son - where is your son?"

In the summer it was usual for us to accompany my husband for his ship inspections. The worst incident happened while touring the city of Athens where a herd of gypsy children stealthily trailed away with little David in between them amidst the mass of people crossing the sidewalk. Only the eagle eyes of a young man sitting in the upstairs floor observing the act and running to catch him saved our son from disappearing forever.

Upon our return to Israel from our travel abroad we asked our friend, N., to please call and ask the tsaddik what was the meaning of all these dangerous occurrences in David's life? The rebbe's reply was nothing short of amazing: he wanted to know our son's middle name. We explained that we gave him that name in honor of Ariel's uncle that fell to the Nazis during the war. The rabbi was visibly concerned and directed us to change the child's name immediately. It is history that Ariel's uncle was an army surgeon. Dr. Michel Goldman had died before his time and was a sacrifice of the war – no child should be named after someone who died unnaturally or before his time. Our rebbe had never known the names of anyone in Ariel's family. Yet we understood that this is the work of a true kabbalist. We agreed to do what was necessary and this is what saved the life of our son.

David's final seal and what protected him was the fierce independence that seemed to rule his actions. Like his mentor the tsaddik, he ate no fruits or vegetables out of season or food that might be questionable. Of course we never understood the meaning of these actions and it took an explanation from our rebbe to calm our nerves.

Two nights before his *halakeh* (cutting the hair at 3 years old) was to take place (the date that was actually his Hebrew birth date) David, all by himself, took scissors and cut the right side of his hair while looking at a mirror. When his sisters caught him in the action they were alarmed and upset. If he cut his hair, they thought, then there might not be a halakeh!

We couldn't bring ourselves to punish him because I don't believe that he even remembered that he was having a hair-cutting ceremony. The tzaddik explained to N. that his actions were ruled by higher powers. This did not require profound explanations – the little boy had his own internal clock and knew when the time had come to cut his hair. The rebbe assured us that he would complete the official cutting of his hair in his synagogue in Jerusalem.

When David passed his 3rd birthday, we finally began to breathe easier. Had it not been for the rebbe's wise counsel, we might not have been able to interpret these events. As time passed we were able to understand that the tsaddik was very connected to our son. However, I want to say that even today we have never understood why we were gifted with such love and kindness from a rabbi whose most important task lay in looking after the well-being and safety of his entire country - Israel.

Our gratitude to the heavens is a daily affair, even though many years have passed since Rabbi Yitzhak Kaduri left our world, he remains part of our world and we are reminded of his kindness when we see our son every day.

Rabbi Itzhak Kaduri, Sgan Hamekubalim, z'l and
Rabbi Ralph Z. Glixman, z'l at the Installation of a Torah at our Merkaz Ruhanit in Ra'anana,, November 15, 1995

Ha Rav Itzhak Kaduri, z'l doing the blessings for welcome the Sepher Torah, November 15, 1995

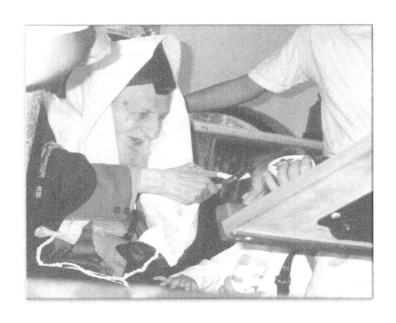

HaRav Kaduri, z'l performing the "halakeh" for our son,
D. Goldman, September 1997

The Rabbanit Dorit Kaduri's blessing after the Halakeh, September 1997

HaRav Kaduri, z'l at our Hannukat Beit, November 1996

HaRav and my husband Ariel, doing the Blessings for the House, November 1996

Our dear friend, Mrs. "R", Mrs. Rabbia, and Rabbanit Marcel, great-grandaughter of the Hacham Ben Ish Chai,
Teacher and mentor to the Tzaddik Rabbi Kaduri
November, 1996

FULFILLED AND COMPLETE

Bringing Healing and Solace to Others

In the years that followed, between 1996 to 1999, we were busy raising our family, working hard, and also doing much learning. I had decided to return to school and explore holistic and oriental medicine. There was a big movement in the country and schools and institutes of natural medicine were starting up every month. Some of the Israeli experts in the field had traveled to China and came back bolstered by the support and mentorship they had received in Asia. So everyone was big on "natural medicine" in Israel and this has remained a steady trend even today.

This matter in fact is what directed me to continue our work with spiritual counseling and merging it with natural medicine. In 1996 both my husband and I entered the Med-Cin Academy in Ramat Gan for the first year of Traditional Chinese Medicine. We completed our studies three years later under another institute but we had always considered that mind-body-medicine was the face of future medicine.

Sadly, around us we saw many people suffering from terminal illnesses, different and aggressive types of cancer, serious types of diabetes, and countless cases of ADD and ADHD. The cases that did break our hearts were those where the cancer had progressed into the third or fourth stage. These were the moments that required caregivers to provide so much more than just medical expertise. Serious or terminal illness demands that some form of spiritual or pastoral care join in with the palliative care that brings relief from pain and suffering. We worked with these cases carefully and as sensitively as possible. With some individuals the work succeeded, with some it did not. We had been fortunate to be under the wing of our rebbe and so we determined that the next opportunity that presented itself we would open our home up to anyone that needed to see Rabbi Yitzhak Kaduri. In September of 1996, we celebrated the move to a new apartment. We opened our home and the ceremonies to anyone that asked. Among many guests, there were at least two women; one suffering from breast cancer and another one praying for a baby. Both received blessings from the tsaddik. The joy of pregnancy blessed one of them but sadly the other lady succumbed to the final stages of cancer.

We asked Rabbanit Dorit, the tsaddik's wife why this was so? Why is it that the rabbi could bless two people and only one would heal completely? She thoughtfully replied that the rabbi's job was to put before the Creator all the requests. No one, however, knew the time of his parting and what would be the final judgment for each one of our souls. Some patients succeeded in using their time wisely and appreciated every moment of life and some were just not strong enough to endure the suffering. Standing by and watching this amazing and heart-rending process taught us much about the importance of life, of gratitude, and the positive power of the mind. We learned that even if someone's life was counted by days, even those precious days should be used to brighten the lives and hopes of others.

Respect for his Mentor and Teacher

On that particular "hannukat bait" in 1996 our friend N. had promised that she would be bringing to the celebration a very special person. We knew nothing about the lady in question but were soon to be amazed by the visit. Through the door entered N. accompanied by a young woman (in her 40's) together with her mother, a small lady with large eyes wearing glasses, a simple head covering and modestly dressed. To our welcome and greeting she smiled demurely and nodded her head. We soon learned the background of this special lady because suddenly from the other side of the room we heard a commotion.

Our tsaddik was asking to be helped up and to usher the small lady to him. This giant of a sage was showing an unusual level of happiness and respect for this elderly lady, greeting and blessing her as she approached him. She humbly nodded and blessed him back.

It was later that N. explained that the great-granddaughter of the well-known rabbi, the Ben Ish-Chai of Iraq, was in our midst. We showed her to a place of honor at the woman's table and later showed her some of the books that we had been studying from her great-grandfather's writings. Out of respect for her 'yichus', we called her rabbanit. So excited were we that such a wonderful person was taking part in our celebration that we asked her to sign her great-grandfather - the Ben Ish-Chai's books. She was happy to do so. It seems that N. shared with her about the work that we'd been doing in the last few years because her dedication and blessings to us concerned "continuing to bring light to many".

We were amazed because we had not at any time exchanged any information or talked about our center. It is my conviction that even the progeny of sages and kabbalists are illuminated in their own fashion. Rabbanit Marcel, great-granddaughter of the Gaon Ben Ish-Chai, was just this way. What of course constantly opened our eyes to the humility of the sage Rabbi Yitzhak Kaduri was the fact that he rose to show respect and recognize a descendant of one of his first masters and teachers, the Ben Ish Chai. We were reminded by Rabbanit Dorit Kaduri's constant expression about never counting on honors or tributes from others as a sign of our success. She always repeated an old biblical saying, "we are food for the worms." It alludes to the prayer that we read in "Shaviti" which says the following: "Know before whom you stand, the King of kings, know where you are headed and where you came from (to the grave to be food for the worms and born from a bitter drop). Even moments of such privilege in meeting these great but humble beings reflected in them a gentle simplicity.

On this occasion the rebbe chose to bless our children privately in a separate room away from the eyes of all guests and participants. Each of our children in turn approached the sage and received a blessing for his or her life and each time it ended with his well-known chuckle.

My husband and I felt nothing but eternal gratitude, first for our friend in helping us set this day for the benefit of our neighbors but also for the highlights of the day: the rebbe's presence in our home, and what would remain forever in our hearts - his love.

His Work and Teachings

The work that my husband and I mostly focused on was in raising the level of mindfulness and awareness in people both from a spiritual and religious perspective. Even if holistic medicine touted that all healing begins in the mind, this was an enormous task. Belief is a personal thing. My present life is testimony to those principles. Yes, it is a valid concept that there is much that I can change to improve the quality of my life, but there is also so much more that I am required to accept and embrace. The task of minding the "mind" is enormous and the tsaddik always counseled against giving oxygen to any negativity.

Rabbi Kaduri saw anger as the strongest aspect of *"yetzer harah" (evil inclination)* and I believe through his teachings, he suffocated that aspect in any person that came to see him. It was typical for him to look at you and smile while he was reflecting on your name. Who knows what the angels were telling him? Who knows what he saw behind each person's façade? Still, every person was received with joy, and every pain and suffering was greeted with a blessing. I don't believe that he knew the meaning of the word "impossible". Since he saw everyone's need as important , he never knew how to turn anyone away. On the contrary, it was his assistants that circled around him that had to do that. It was a thankless job but so necessary in order to conserve the centenarian sage's health.

The tsaddik and his wife, Rabbanit Dorit, lived in poverty and humility. Countless times, when my husband traveled abroad he would ask the rebbe through N. if there was anything in particular that he needed? He would chuckle and nod his head but never asked anything for himself. We were amazed at how well known he was even in the non-Jewish communities of Israel.

On one occasion our family traveled to the Druze village of Dalyat el-Carmel and had lunch at one of the oldest family-owned restaurants there. We complimented them on their food and their famous sweets, which are known around the world. The owner asked us where we were from and who was our rebbe? We replied that we followed Rabbi Kaduri. The man jumped up and asked us to stay seated – he wanted to get the village elder to come and meet us. Ariel and I looked at each other in surprise, we didn't know if we were in danger or what had prompted that reaction. From outside an elder Druze gentleman, tall and well into his 70's came in and introduced himself. He asked if we would be seeing our rebbe anytime soon and we assured him that we visited our rabbi periodically. He presented us with a large box carrying a hand-made snow-white mantle of pure wool for which the Druze are famous for making. The elder asked us to ensure that we would present this to the tsaddik in his name and he wrote a small note dedicated to the rabbi. Even at a distance, the rebbe's influence blessed our ways!

Another time, there was a very wealthy Turkish gentleman whose young daughter (around 10 years old) had been diagnosed with cancer. After exhausting all the possibilities for a cure in their own country, the family was left with little hope. Someone must have told them about the rebbe so they immediately called the yeshiva in Jerusalem and reached out to the rabbi's grandson via the Turkish Jewish community. They wanted to come and receive a blessing from the rabbi for their young daughter's health and they were willing to pay any price. They had the means to travel in their own jet to Israel. The rabbi's family and assistants were inclined to refuse the request and said so to the rebbe. They protested to no avail, the tsaddik had made up his mind. He simply stated, "If they come to my door for a blessing, who am I to turn them away?" And so it was that the little girl was brought to the tsaddik and a blessing and scroll was prepared by the rebbe in her name. Within the short time of less than a month the Turkish family called back to let the rebbe know that their daughter's brain tumor had all but disappeared miraculously. They had no words with which to thank the rebbe.

Stories like these abound in and out of Israel and we were fortunate to witness only a few. They were all marvelous feats of man's faith in G-d and his messenger, yet my husband and I had seen firsthand how he had saved my life. I required no tales of miracles – I was living proof.
It can be said, however, that the power of his words was legendary.

We recall the time when he visited our home in Ra'anana and as he was getting ready to climb into the van to leave a young professional journalist was trying to photograph him. The rebbe turned around and said "*Lo tetzalem!*" – meaning "you will not photograph". My husband watched as the journalist shot the photo but the flash didn't go off. He feverishly put in new batteries and continued shooting but to no avail. He finally removed the film and placed a new roll of film in the camera but it still would not shoot! He couldn't believe it – to tell the truth – my husband couldn't believe his eyes either. Had he not seen that little episode, Ariel would have considered it just another tall tale. The van's door slid to a close and the young journalist just stood there, open mouthed, not knowing what had just happened. Yes, we knew first hand that the rebbe's words were powerful. Another time it happened that a devotee of the rabbi's had obtained a special and personally written blessing from the tsaddik. The devotee was counseled never to publish, or to show through photographs or displays any part of the blessing as these were extremely sacred writings and would not withstand the public eye.

There were many devotees that didn't take the warning seriously – others didn't think to test the rebbe's warning and guarded their blessings with their life. Just how powerful these blessings were was proved by the public. One devotee thought he was being clever and when he was interviewed allowed the journalist to photograph the framed blessing. Well, next day, when the blessing showed up in all the newspapers, the rebbe was seriously upset. Not because of what it revealed but because of the simple fact that all newspapers final destination is where? – the wastebasket. Needless to say, that devotee ended up having legal problems, great financial loss and business troubles that were beyond his comprehension. It was known that events like this happened every so often and sadder still was the fact that it would be a long time before the devotee gained the rebbe's trust again.

The upside of the rebbe's blessings were also quite visible in the Israeli press more than once. At least twice in our experience, we read of two separate cases where business men that owned a falafel and shawarma restaurant and another one owning a food stand that had gone to see the rabbi and asked for blessings for a profitable business. Even though the blessings were out of sight, they had hung a portrait of the tsaddik on one of the walls of the restaurant. In both cases the restaurant and stand had either been badly burned or destroyed yet the wall with the tsaddik's portrait was still standing and the owners were able to rebuild their businesses with minimal losses. Amazing, right? These are things that you need to see to believe.

Rabbi Yitzhak Kaduri fled from publicity and it is known that he would rarely glance at journalists and photographers. Kabbalists know the perils of the ego and they rarely allowed any type of promotion. Their lives are dedicated to humility, prayer and service of the Eternal. It was clear that the lure of grandeur and popularity did not fool or attract them. These kabbalists attempted to live holy lives and represented a tight circle that was and has always been difficult to break.

Where is "the driver's wife"?

In the last years leading up to 2000, right before we were forced to take a sabbatical to the US, we visited the rabbi a number of times. These were difficult times for everyone. Worldwide economies were struggling. There was enough evidence obvious to us as Ariel and his partner's firm of twelve years was slowly going aground. Most of the companies that hired their security services and consulting were now establishing their own in-house security departments. While they still relied on the consulting side of the firm, this was not enough to hire and maintain the staff of more than 200 officers on their payroll at any given time. As such, Ariel and his partner, Y., a very nice man parted ways.

Our visits to the rebbe's kollel were meant mostly to uplift our morale. We were at our wits end and didn't really know what the future would bring. There was so much uncertainty and I think that the same could have been said of those years in Israel. The intifada was at its peak and so many lost their lives for the simplest reasons, merely because we were Jews trying to live in harmony with our neighbors everywhere.

I was not feeling my best. I had just lost a baby and my spirits were low. Ariel called our friend N. and asked her if we could see the rebbe. We needed his blessing and just being in his holy presence was enough for us. We weren't looking for a better business deal or for a bigger house, all we wanted was health, wellbeing and peace of mind. N. as always was very supportive of us even during hard times and agreed that it would be a great idea to go see the rebbe. That morning we were told to visit him in the small flat in the Bukharin quarters, two blocks away from the

Nahalat Yitzhak kollel where he usually studied and received the public. This is the where all the people came to stand in line to see him. Sometimes they would stand there for hours on end just to get their names on the list. On this particular morning the rebbe was alone in his prayer room. His grandson, Yossi, welcomed us in. It was customary for me to stay outside in the hall while my husband would come in to greet him first. Out of respect for his age and the fact that the sage was an elder, my husband would enter with N. and formally greet him.

The tsaddik would either be in deep thoughts or he would be very alert. In more than one occasion, my husband states, the rebbe would inquire as to my health and wellbeing. The tsaddik asked my husband "and where is the driver's wife?" My husband assured him that I was outside and the rebbe asked him to bring me in. These were moments when I felt lower than the dust under an ant's foot. My throat would become dry and I would have a knot in my stomach. I would look at his hands in awe and reverence but could never bring myself to look into his eyes. The moment that I sat in the chair beside him – it was as if I were sitting beside a bright pulsating sun.

Tears would stream down my cheeks as I whispered to him my concerns, my worries as a mother, my request for a strong healthy recovery, and my hopes that our future would be a safe one outside of Eretz Hakodesh. This scenario repeated itself many times during the last year before we left Israel but the rebbe assured us each time that this was for the best. He encouraged me to continue studying Torah and the holy writings. He admonished me to never leave my work and that this would be the *segoula* (protection) for our family – helping others and strengthening their faith in the Torah. The tsaddik promised that marvelous things were ahead of us. Most importantly – he encouraged us to never lose faith.

The rebbe was right. In February of the year 2000, when we returned to the US and landed in Simi Valley, California, there I gave birth to a beautiful baby girl whom we named Sarah. There also, I was offered the wonderful opportunity to teach Hebrew and Judaic Studies at the West Valley Hebrew Academy in Tarzana.

Many more wonderful events occured in California. We had the honor and privilege of meeting and learning with another revered rebbe, Rabbi Laibl Wolf, a kabbalist rabbi and disciple of Rabbi Shlomo Carlebach, when he visited the Simi Valley community. Additionally, in Simi Valley, we also had the privilege of welcoming into our home Rabbanit Simi Abuhazera, the wife of the beloved Baba Sali of Morocco.

Yes, it was a year full of marvelous surprises and blessings from one end of the year to the other. For years to come the rebbe's words reverberated in our ears. Never lose faith.

THE TZADDIK'S PROMISE OF THE "MOSCHIACH"

This is a simple recounting of many of the things that we heard while we were close to Rabbi Yitzhak Kaduri's circle. The times that we would go and visit his kollel at night and have tea with the tsaddik and his wife, our friend N. also did some listening.

It is said that the rebbe shared with those close to him that he had already met the "moshiach". He expressed confidence that the coming of the redeemer would occur during our lifetime. It was in these moments when he bolstered our confidence the most. Israel had endured many attacks and for many years, the Second Intifada was an abnormal strain on the Israeli citizens. We did not like to live with this situation, but we were made stronger by it. Our own personal experience attests to the challenges of remaining calm and positive while under terrorist attacks in the inner city.

My mother-in-law, Claire Gollan, lived at 41 Dizengoff. Ariel's grandparents, father and uncles came from Russia through Romania and Belgium and decided to construct an apartment building on the main street of Dizengoff. This property was constructed in the 1930's and housed all of my husband's family. When Ariel's father passed away in 1989, Mama Claire, as we all called her, was living alone in her small flat. On March 4, 1996, a suicide bomber blew himself up outside of the Dizengoff shopping center.

The bomb killed 14 Israelis. The explosion was so powerful that it blew out the window glass of Mama Claire's apartment. We were blocks away from the mall and felt the booming and loud explosion. It was a neighbor that called our cell phone from Claire's apartment to say that, although she was safe, all the windows in the apartment had imploded and shards of glass were everywhere, inside and outside of the apartment and on the balconies! It was clear that she could not stay in the apartment alone. The carnage outside the mall was heartbreaking and being in this climate of terror only made us more committed to seek peace – at any cost.

The tsaddik however saw beyond the turmoil and loss. With every loss, with every attack, he would restrain the masses from losing sight of what was important. We, the Jewish people, were not like them. We did not send martyrs to their death for the sake of retaliation. As a matter of fact, the whole concept of suicide was and still remains to this day contrary to everything we believe in. Our prophet Moses ordered us to always "choose life!". And because of this, we believed that all these trials would soon be over. In September of 2005, when Israel established the Unilateral Disengagement of the Gaza strip it was because we didn't want to continue losing lives on the borders of the country.

When we pulled out of Gaza and left them to construct their own lives, this too was a hopeful step for the Arabs independence. I recall standing at the highway intersections on GEHA road, together with our friends and neighbors demonstrating with the majority of the modern religious communities in the cities that the government let go in order to receive something in return.

The following month, October of 2005, the tsaddik Rabbi Yitzhak Kaduri, during the fast of Yom Kippur, fasted and pleaded with the heavens for the safety and return of all the Jews to Israel. It is said that he had seen the soul of the "moschiach" attach itself to a person in Israel.

Redemption, it was said, was on its way.

FOREVER WITH US

Defender of Israel
His passing on January 28, 2006

Our memories of that day are blurry. We had been in touch with our friend N. and T. all day long. A few days earlier he had been admitted into the hospital for what seemed like a respiratory infection. We were constantly on the phone with our friend as she explained that there was turmoil and confusion. The rebbe just wanted to go home and his son, Rabbi David and grandson Yossi wanted to make sure he was strong enough to recuperate. Then, he was sent home and his health worsened. He was having difficulties breathing and so they discovered that the rebbe had pneumonia. The rebbe was taken back into the hospital but there wasn't an artificial respirator that perhaps would have saved his life. At 10:00pm on the evening of January 28th, 2006, our tsaddik took his last breath. An announcement was made on Israeli television amidst weeping in the streets. Huge groups of *haredi* (orthodox) men gathered outside the hospital, and outside many locations including his yeshiva Nahalat Yitzhak, all of them whispered what would be the fate of Israel now that the tsaddik was gone?

It is said that over 300,000 people took part in the tsaddik's funeral. Jerusalem was closed off and N. and her husband in Tel Aviv, and our family in Ra'anana sat in front of the television that morning to watch the final march to the rebbe's resting place. A sea of people moved as in waves, undulating through the streets as if in a daze making their way to the "house of life", the cemetery of Har Hamenuchot in Jerusalem.

One of the greatest rabbis of our generation had dedicated his entire life to his people and to his country. His prayers and his words of wisdom had brought peace between different sectors of the Jewish orthodox community. When he spoke concerning a law, everyone listened but, it was known that as a rule he barely spoke.

To the last moment our rebbe, Rabbi Yitzhak Kaduri, was conscious and fully aware of everything around him. The tsaddik had embodied his many teachers' counsel - to save his speech only for holy matters. His utterances were powerful. His humble and simple life belied the wonders and miracles he set into motion everyday of his life and after his passing, the many miracles would eventually come to light.

THE TSADDIK'S VISIT IN A DREAM

THE VISIT

Throughout our youngest daughter's life, Sarah has often complained that she never personally met the rebbe or experienced his blessings the way her siblings had. Even when we assured her that his blessings fill our house and home, and that every step that we have ever taken seemed to be guided by the Almighty's hand together with the tsaddik, I suppose that will never suffice for a young and vibrant spirit like our daughter. Yet, Sarah has an old soul. Her love of the Torah, her commitment to the mitzvahs and to "saving" every Jew, no matter how confused or misguided they are – is unique to Sarah's nature. Unlike many girls her age, she is emotionally balanced and considerate and loving of both the old and the young. She exudes joy and laughter because she sees the light in every human being. Her spiritual sensitivity is a gift that we recognize as coming from the blessings we received when I was carrying her before we returned to the US in the year 2000.

We believe that the tsaddik touched her through his "kavanot" or intentions. We are certain of this because with her birth many blessings came flowing forth. Sarah was born in California during the time that we worked at the West Valley Hebrew Academy in Tarzana. Her birth was welcomed and embraced by many that when I began working as a teacher, we didn't need to get a babysitter for her during the day. We were permitted to bring her as a newborn in her stroller and she would be parked in the administrative offices of the school. She was held, coddled, and fed throughout the day by the loving teachers that frequented the office (aside from my periodic visits in between class time). So, Sarah was almost "communally" raised in her first year of life. The rabbis would come and go throughout the day and there wasn't a time when she wasn't picked up and brought into the conversation. Sarah wasn't a needy child and she seemed to know where she was because the staff barely heard her cry but – she was always listening.

The blessings that came directly after her birth were signs for us that the rebbe's influence was always with our family. One of many examples was the fact that my husband Ariel was chosen for one of the most important positions of his life when he served as Security Coordinator for the G-8 meeting in Europe in July of 2001.

These past fifteen years have only been an extension of those beginnings. So, I was not surprised when on the 21st of January, 2015, one Wednesday evening as I returned home, Sarah wanted to share with me her dream from the night before. Sarah's dreams are extremely clear and as a matter of record they are most often prophetic in nature – even about small matters. This time the dream was about someone that she had always wanted to personally meet.

"I entered a white hall filled with light and down that hall there were many white doors. I walked further in and chose a door to my right where I entered into a room. To one side there was a beautiful wooden wide table that served as a desk or bimah and on it the tsaddik was reading from a book. As I entered the room he looked up and smiled. I looked to the other side of the room and saw three rabbis sitting on chairs while at the center of the circle I again saw the tsaddik, Rabbi Kaduri, with a book on his lap. He beckoned me with his hand to come closer to his side and read from the book. When I tried to read from it I felt my throat tighten while tears were streaming from my cheeks. I wanted to read but I was in awe of what the book contained and shook my head indicating that I didn't feel worthy to touch or read the book. The other sages around him were very distinctive in physical features. One had a large turban around his head, a dark grey white beard and was dressed in a robe with silver and black on it. The third rabbi around the tsaddik had a flat and round white hat on his head, a long white beard and he too was shining with a completely white robe. The last rabbi in the circle had a white kippa on his head and had a short beard. They directed me to sit beside them as they were reading out loud with pointers in their hands. I could not remember what they were saying but as they spoke I saw letters flying from the books into the air in front of me. From time to time I would look up at the tsaddik and saw him smiling at me and nodding his head. He wasn't upset that I had refused to read from the book but I felt loved and embraced by these sages that I have never seen before. At some point in time we must have been singing something sweet but it was a melody that I cannot remember. I dreamed this dream continuously throughout the night and finally nearing morning I saw myself get up and turn to say "shalom" to the rabbis. I turned to leave and exited through another door opposite the one that I entered."

After listening to Sarah's dream I got up to show her the pictures of some of the rabbis that I thought perhaps she had met in her dream. The sage that Sarah described with the turban was in fact identical to the image of the tsaddik Ben Ish Chai, the sage with the flat round hat, it seemed, looked very much like the kabbalist and tsaddik, Rabbi Mordechai Sharaby. The rabbi with the white kippa still remains unrecognized even after many months.

I would not dare interpret a dream that to me seemed complete. This privilege was uniquely Sarah's and as such I could only say that it was our belief that perhaps the tsaddikim were visiting her a few days before Rabbi Yitzhak Kaduri's anniversary of his passing – a time when holy and very spiritually powerful souls have the permission to visit the earth.

When I reviewed the Hebrew calendar, the date of Sarah's dream was exactly on the anniversary of the rebbe's passing. There was to my view, nothing to add. Also, when I checked the dates in Rabbi Abraham Abulafia's writings on dreams, it was commented that on the 28th day of the month "whatever you dream is a blessing for you". We living beings do not need to add or detract to what is already a blessed occurrence. The tsaddik's visit to Sarah was just such an event. I pointed out to Sarah that she could never again complain that she had not met the rebbe as it was clear that he had made her wish come true.

The ways of the Almighty are mysterious and no man can know the what or why of it. Once again Sarah's blessings touch all of us.

LOOKING BACK

I was fortunate to be born to simple, good and hardworking parents. My father was a military man unaffiliated with any religion although his mother, A. Cabrera, was from a Spanish Marrano family. My mother's father was Jewish and her mother was Christian. I only discovered these facts later in my life (at age 41)- when my mother decided to share with me what her mother and grandmother told her as a child. Still, in my childhood there were many signs along the way that an invisible hand had guided my journey back to Judaism.

Before I was born prematurely (8 months) my mother suffered severe eclampsia attacks and the doctors were afraid that both of us would not survive childbirth. Mrs. Crespin, my mother's Jewish best friend and mentor when she arrived from Cuba, suggested to my father that he should choose a different name other than the one he had originally chosen for me. Sara suggested Myriam. When the doctors asked him whom should they try to save he replied that it was in the hands of G-d. Sara volunteered to look after me while my mother was still in a delicate state of health, and so when I was still in the incubator, Sara pinned a golden Star of David to my baby shirt.

Together with my father, Sara would visit me at the nursery to ensure I was thriving. The golden star followed me throughout my childhood. It seemed that Sara's strategy was to confuse the Angel of Death.

At the age of 11, my family moved to Normandy Isle where I attended 6th grade at Treasure Island Elementary. At this time my classmates were getting ready for their bat/bar mitzvahs and so there was a Hebrew class at our school. When I tried to sign up for Sunday school (like everyone else) the rabbi kindly told me that I could not participate. I insisted that I belonged there. He apologized but made it clear that I was not permitted to join my sixth grade classmates in their lessons. Not easily discouraged I then asked if he would allow me to sit outside of the class, under the open windows and listen to the class. The teacher must have been tired of me because he finally took out a chair and let me sit outside to listen to his lessons. I was determined to learn so after walking home with my classmates I made my own Hebrew workbook. I took out my World Book Encyclopedia and cut out the page with the Hebrew alphabet. I practiced writing the letters until I knew them by heart. No one was going to stand in my way of learning, and my mother certainly was supportive of all my efforts.

My family relocated to Chicago due to the economic situation in the late 1970's. When we returned to Miami ten years later I remember telling my parents that I wanted to investigate my Jewish roots and again they were very encouraging of my interest. I only got one chance to meet with an elderly rabbi that served an old synagogue on 12th street near the Roads in Little Havana. The rabbi was very helpful. Based on the information I gave him about my origins he stated that it would take work to learn more about my roots but that even if the Jewish roots came from my maternal grandfather, I still needed to convert. He apologized that he couldn't help me further as the synagogue was being sold to a Baptist church in the coming months and I would have to pursue this matter through another temple.

In 1985 while working at Hospice, Inc., I was privileged to meet a wonderful person. He was the chaplain and rabbi for the Miami Beach patient team: Rabbi Warren Kasztl. When I told him that I was interested in converting he pointed me towards Rabbi R. Glixman, (OBM). The rest is history. Rabbi Ralph Zevulun Glixman, after inquiring my reasons for wanting to convert, asked me to write down everything that I knew about my family. My first rebbe, Rabbi R. Glixman, opened the door to my real life. And, nothing has ever been the same again.

I have known true happiness only through my family, fulfillment through my children and have been lucky enough to have received the guidance from the mouths of humble '*lamed vavniks*" (hidden hachamim of which there are 36 in the entire world). It seems to me that I have never been abandoned by the Almighty - He has always heard my prayers and my tears, blessed and mighty is He. It is this conviction that I try to daily convey to others when they feel alone or dejected.

Three years ago when I decided to pursue rabbinical studies, again I felt that the time was right. It seemed that new horizons were opening up for Jewish orthodox women in this field. My prayers were answered when I read about the first Rabba, Sarah Hurwitz of New Jersey, and how she received her smicha in 2010 from Rabbi Avi Weiss from The Hebrew Institute of Riverdale in the Bronx, NY. I took this milestone as a sign that there was plenty of room for women willing to become spiritual leaders in ways both big and small. Not every woman rabbi needs or wants to lead a "*schul*" (congregation). Sometimes what is needed are female spiritual leaders that are willing to listen to a woman's questions, uncertainties, or worries but always it is important to relate these challenges to the lessons we learn from the Torah. Like the Holocaust victim, Rabbiner Sara Jonas, the first ordained female rabbi in Germany during WWII, I have always felt a deep connection to the Tanach, to its teachings, and particularly to the Book of Psalms, *The Tehillim*.

Weeks before I was to travel to New York for my ordination, again, I meditated on the Lubavitcher Rebbe's letters and asked if this enterprise was blessed from above. The answer that we received could not have been clearer. The reply opened onto a letter the Lubavitcher Rebbe had written to a student who would be celebrating a successful achievement on the anniversary of the first Lubavitcher rebbe's passing. My husband, who is the only one who can read Yiddish, asked me what were the dates of the ordination. When I replied, Ariel showed me that the Lubavitcher rebbe's letter exactly matched the dates of this important event. What were the odds of the dates having matched? I cannot answer that.
If I had the support and love of my family and the way seemed clear for me to proceed with my studies - then what more could I ask of Hashem?

I have always received this from my children and my husband. May Hashem bless my loved ones and fill their lives with health, happiness and success every day. When people ask me how I am doing, I easily respond with Solomon's question:

"Who is the happy man? – He who is happy with his lot." Proverbs

THE REBBE'S LIFE

A Brief Summary of the Rebbe's Life

As biographies go, this section of the book is meant to briefly give you an overview of what is known of the Rabbi Yitzhak Kaduri. The large part of this material can be found under the contributions made on several websites under his name. While I have looked through many sources on the internet, very few articles were written about the rebbe either of his life or after his passing. What might be the most important fact is that this is probably the way he would have wanted things to be.

We know that he was born Katchouri Diba ben Aziza in Baghdad near the turn of the century, but 1902 seems to be the date used by most journalists in their interviews with him. In his youth it is said that Rabbi Kaduri was an excellent student, so much so, that he was permitted to learn the secrets of Kabbalah in his teens – something that is rare and not common with today's yeshiva students. He studied under the Ben Ish Chai (Rabbi Yosef Chaim of Baghdad) at Zilka Yeshivah in Baghdad.

In 1923 the rebbe, upon the advice of the elders of Baghdad, left for Eretz Israel – the Holy Land, at the time was known as the British Mandate of Palestine. The elders hoped that his piety and scholarship would protect the delicate state of Jerusalem. There he studied at Shoshanim LeDavid Yeshiva for Kabbalists from Iraq. He also studied Talmud and rabbinical law at Porat Yosef Yeshiva together with other greats such as Rabbi Ezra Attiya, and Rabbi Saliman Eliyahu (the father of the Chief Sephardic Rabbi Mordechai Eliyahu).

In 1934 Rabbi Kaduri moved with his family into the Old City where the Yeshiva Porat Yosef provided him with an apartment. They also gave him the job of binding the yeshiva's books and copying other rare manuscripts in their library. The actual manuscripts remained in Rabbi Kaduri's own library. It is known that he had a photographic memory and knew the Talmud, Rashi and Tosafot commentaries by heart. In 1948 during the Arab-Israeli War the Porat Yosef Yeshiva was set on fire by the Jordanians invading the Old City. Rabbi Kaduri tried to save as many manuscripts as possible and smuggled them to Beit El Yeshiva. It is known that he had memorized the writings of Yitzhak Luria, the founder of modern Kabbalah. When the leader of the kabbalists, Rabbi Efraim Hakohen, passed away in 1989, the remaining kabbalists unanimously appointed Rabbi Kaduri as their head.

We know that the rabbi did not publish any works but many books of prayer were given his blessing and endorsement.

Although he may have blessed the many initiatives of other devotees and rabbi scholars, he himself only allowed kabbalah students to touch the works of the ancients. Rabbi Kaduri was against teaching Kabbalah to non-Jews and was not an adherent of "practical Kabbalah". Although he wrote many amulets, and gave many blessings and prophecies, what he was most known for was his prophecies.

Rabbi Kaduri loved his country and although many politicians tried to utilize his powers for their political interests, in the end - all these fell by the wayside. One particular aspect of his character is that he commanded secrecy and reverence for what he revealed to his followers. Many celebrities and wealthy men lost their fame or fortunes for violating the respect that was required of his guidance and blessings.

The rebbe's life was one of humility, modesty and poverty. He widowed from his first wife, Rabbanit Sara, in 1989 and remarried Rabbanit Dorit in 1993, a ba'alat teshuva. His cloaks may have been frayed and few but they were of little importance to the man that prayed night and day for the peace and well being of his people and his country, Israel, the Holy Land. Since my husband and I and our children were living witnesses to the life he led and the greatness of the rebbe's soul, we can attest to the fact that nothing of material value ever distracted his attention.

As holy men go, the rebbe was the holiest, most erudite yet simplest human being we have ever met. Yet, when he stood to pray and meditate – his prayers could last well into hours – and not one follower would breathe or move until the rebbe returned from his meditations and awakened.

His modest wife, Rabbanit Dorit always made the same remark and today, more than ever, I believe that she heard this from Rabbi Yitzhak Kaduri: "We are all food for the worms…..".

For the rest of our lives we will always miss our earthly teacher and master.